Horse

APPALOOSA HORSES

ELIZABETH NOLL

BLACK
RABBIT
BOOKS

Bolt is published by Black Rabbit Books
P.O. Box 3263, Mankato, Minnesota, 56002.
www.blackrabbitbooks.com
Copyright © 2019 Black Rabbit Books

Marysa Storm, editor; Catherine Cates &
Grant Gould, designers; Omay Ayres, photo
researcher

Library of Congress Cataloging-in-Publication Data
Names: Noll, Elizabeth, author.
Title: Appaloosa horses / by Elizabeth Noll.
Description: Mankato, Minnesota : Black Rabbit Books, [2019] | Series:
Bolt. Horse crazy | Audience: Ages 9-12. | Audience: Grades 4-6. |
Includes bibliographical references and index.
Identifiers: LCCN 2017036086 (print) | LCCN 2017044611 (ebook) |
ISBN 9781680725292 (e-book) | ISBN 9781680724134 (library binding) |
ISBN 9781680727074 (paperback)
Subjects: LCSH: Appaloosa horse–Juvenile literature. | Horses–Juvenile
literature.
Classification: LCC SF293.A7 (ebook) | LCC SF293.A7 N65 2019 (print) |
DDC 636.1/3–dc23
LC record available at https://lccn.loc.gov/2017036086

Printed in China. 3/18

Image Credits

CONTENTS

CHAPTER 1

Meet the

APPALOOSA

An Appaloosa walks slowly around the arena. The spotted horse can move quickly, but that's not what its rider needs. This Appaloosa is a **therapy** horse. People with **disabilities** ride it.

This Appaloosa is good at its job. Its steps are regular and steady. Smooth movements help its rider relax. She smiles and laughs.

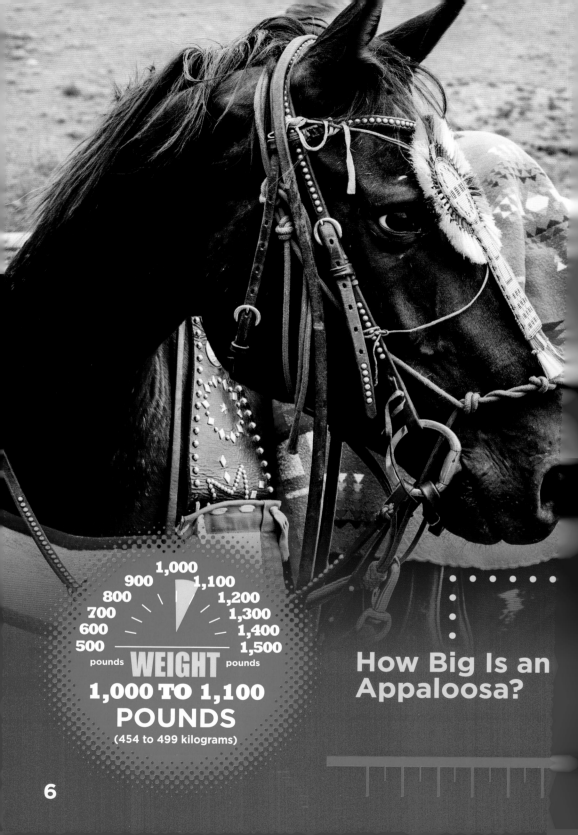

1,000
900   1,100
800   1,200
700   1,300
600   1,400
500   1,500
pounds **WEIGHT** pounds

1,000 TO 1,100 POUNDS
(454 to 499 kilograms)

How Big Is an Appaloosa?

A Bold History

Appaloosas have worked with humans for hundreds of years. Around the 1700s, the **Nez Perce** began **breeding** Appaloosas. They wanted smart, fast, and strong horses. Today's gentle Appaloosas still have these traits.

HEIGHT
at withers
57 TO 64
INCHES
5 to 163 centimeters)

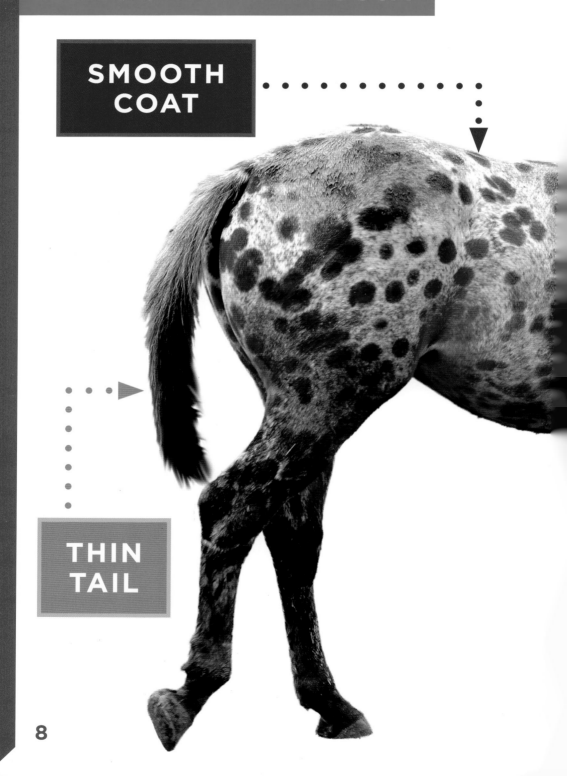

SMOOTH COAT

THIN TAIL

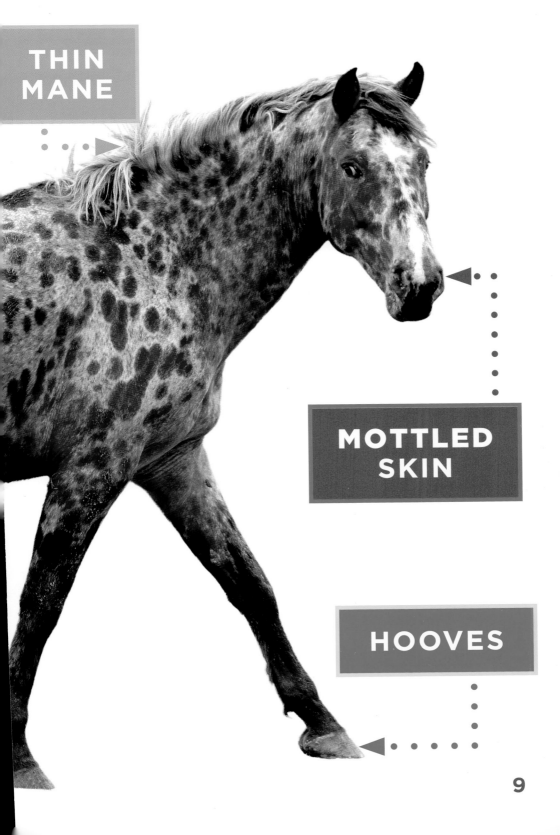

THIN
MANE

MOTTLED
SKIN

HOOVES

9

CHAPTER 2

Features of an APPALOOSA

Appaloosas have many different coat patterns. No two horses have the same spot pattern. Appaloosas have a variety of body types too. Some are tall and thin. Others are more muscular.

COMPARING HEIGHTS

68 TO 72 INCHES
(173 TO 183 CM)

60 TO 68 INCHES
(152 TO 173 CM)

CLYDESDALE

THOROUGHBRED

57 TO 64 INCHES (145 TO 163 CM)	UP TO 42 INCHES (107 CM)	LESS THAN 34 INCHES (86 CM)

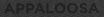

APPALOOSA

SHETLAND PONY

MINIATURE

APPALOOSAS' COAT STYLES

Appaloosas have a variety of coat patterns.

BLANKET

LEOPARD

SNOWFLAKE

FROST

MARBLE

13

Many Appaloosas are **energetic.**

Appaloosas' Personalities

Most Appaloosas are calm, gentle, and quiet. People also consider these horses to be very smart. They like to please their owners.

CHAPTER 3

Appaloosas' USES

Appaloosas are easy to train.
Because they're easy to work with,
they have many uses. People use them
for racing, trail riding, and working.
These strong horses are good for
herding cows.

Appaloosas
in Western Competitions

barrel racing

horse and rider race around three barrels

reining

rider leads the horse through a series of moves

Showing Appaloosas

Owners also use Appaloosas in horse shows and other contests. These horses may be used for jumping and other English events, such as **dressage**. Other Appaloosas compete in western events.

cutting

horse and rider remove cow from herd and block its way back

CHAPTER 4

CARING
for an Appaloosa

Appaloosas need daily care, including feeding and exercising. They also need regular **grooming**. Their coats must be rubbed and brushed to remove dirt. Their hooves must be cleaned out too.

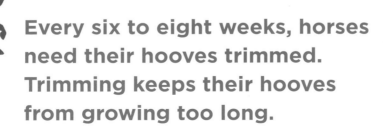

Every six to eight weeks, horses need their hooves trimmed. Trimming keeps their hooves from growing too long.

Eating and Exercising

Horses in pastures **graze** most of the day. Not all horses live in pastures, though. Some live in stables. Stabled horses need about two meals each day. Their meals are mostly hay. All horses need fresh water.

Stabled horses also need daily exercise. Appaloosas should get 30 to 60 minutes. Owners can exercise their horses by riding them.

Appaloosas often live 25 to 30 years.

Appaloosa
LIFE CYCLE

Newborns don't have the same coat patterns they'll have as adults.

FOAL

Older horses often have more health problems.

ADOLESCENT

Most horses can be ridden at two years old.

ADULT

Appaloosas are considered adults at four or five years old.

SENIOR

Horse Health

Appaloosas are usually healthy. But each horse is different. Some have no night vision. Their pink noses can get sunburned too. Older horses might become **swaybacked**.

• • • • • • • • • • • • • • • • • • • •

Up to 25 percent of Appaloosas have a disease that causes night blindness. These horses can't see anything in the dark.

UP TO **1** IN **4** APPALOOSAS HAVE NIGHT BLINDNESS

A Spotted Friend

Appaloosas are famous for their spotted coats. But they're more than just good looking. These horses are strong and smart. They make excellent friends.

GLOSSARY

adolescent (ad-oh-LES-uhnt)—a young person or animal that is developing into an adult

breeding (BREED-ing)—the process by which young animals are produced by their parents

disability (dis-uh-BIL-i-tee)—a condition that damages or limits a person's abilities

dressage (dreh-SAHZH)—a competition in which horses perform special movements in response to signals from their riders

energetic (en-er-JET-ik)—having a lot of energy

graze (GRAYZ)—to feed on growing grass or herbs

grooming (GROOM-ing)—to clean and care for someone or something

mottled (MOT-ld)—covered with colored spots or blotches

Nez Perce (NEZ PURS)—American Indian people of Idaho, Washington, and Oregon

swayback (SWEY-bak)—having an abnormally hollow or sagging back

therapy (THER-uh-pee)—the treatment of physical or mental illnesses

BOOKS

Dell, Pamela. *Appaloosas.* All about Horses. New York: AV2 by Weigl, 2017.

Jackson, Tom. *Horses around the World.* Animals around the World. Mankato, MN: Smart Apple Media, 2015.

Meister, Cari. *Appaloosa Horses.* Favorite Horse Breeds. Mankato, MN: Amicus/Amicus Ink, 2019.

WEBSITES

Appaloosa
www.britannica.com/animal/Appaloosa

Horse
www.ducksters.com/animals/horse.php

Horse
www.nationalgeographic.com/animals/ mammals/h/horse/

INDEX